BRIAN ADAMS

INN LOVE: An Introduction to the Bed and Breakfast Business for Aspiring Innkeepers

This book was professionally typeset on Reedsy.
Find out more at reedsy.com

Contents

A Warm Welcome to the Cozy and Charming World of Bed and Breakfasts

In the cluttered world of choices, where one might ponder whether to become a florist, a librarian, a teacher, or perhaps a lion tamer, there lies a path less trodden but infinitely cozy - the life of a bed and breakfast innkeeper. It is a life that sings the praises of warm welcomes, crisp linens, and serving the kind of breakfasts that your guests wish mornings lasted until at least three in the afternoon!

Welcome! I am your guide on this delightful journey, a journey I embarked on myself and spent 11 years as a successful owner/innkeeper in the mountains of northwest North Carolina. This is not just a book; it is a heartfelt invitation to consider a life that starts with quietly beginning the cooking routine for your guests' breakfast each day and ends with the clinking of coffee cups, lots of laughter, and a new day of adventure ahead. I have been where you are now - standing at the crossroads of curiosity and dream-chasing, wondering if the world of bed and breakfasts is as enchanting as it seems. I will let you in on a little secret: **it is**.

Until I stood on my front porch at the B & B on the first day of opening, I was not sure. When I said the magic words in greeting my guests, "Welcome, friends!", I knew then that I was in the right place.

But let us not get ahead of ourselves. Like the best of journeys, we must start at the beginning. I was once a nine-to-fiver, a familiar face in the daily grind, working at a large five-story office building in school district administration in Florida. I was set to retire at the end of June that year when I bought the Bed and Breakfast. I promise, it was a life changer for me.

Now, as it turned out, after having spent more than a decade being an innkeeper, I have gathered a treasure trove of experiences, insights, and quite a few recipes for scones, egg casseroles, and biscuits with gravy that I am eager to share with you (in the next book, however!).

And might I remind you, I made money in this business too! This, my new friends, is a chance for me to give back some of the information and ideas I learned along the way during this delightful journey and provide you with a starting point and road map for you to follow should you, too, decide to jump in!

This is your compass in the world of bed and breakfast hospitality. It is a world that demands a special blend of skills - part host, part chef, and part mind-reader, with a dash of gardening thrown in for good measure. I will guide you through the nuances of selecting the right property, creating an ambiance and atmosphere that guests fall in love with, and tweaking the art of breakfast cuisine that I am sure makes even the simplest eggs that you make now taste like a culinary masterpiece. Believe it or not, it is fun even at 6 a.m.

We will also delve into the less glamorous but equally important aspects - like managing bookings and understanding the legalities of running a business from your home. I will share a few stories - the good, the bad, and the ones that are too funny not to tell - from my years of experience. These are the lessons I learned the hard way so that you won't have to. And here is a real word of advice: Know your audience—your guests—and treat them to the fun you have had along the way!

Perhaps you are at the brink of retirement, looking for a change of pace and scenery as I was. Or maybe you are simply seeking a life that replaces conference calls with conversations over freshly brewed coffee. Whatever your reasons, this book is your first step towards that dream.

Owning a bed and breakfast is not just about offering a place to sleep; it is about creating a home away from home. It is about understanding that every guest arrives with a story and helping them leave with another one to tell. It is about the joy of seeing the same faces return year after year because what you offer is more than just a stay; it is an experience.

As we progress through this book, I will share the secrets that make a bed and breakfast truly special. From the art of perfecting the guest experience to a bit about the financial know-how of running a real business successfully, each chapter is designed to bring you closer to your dream.

By the end of our journey together, I hope to leave you not just informed but inspired. Inspired to open your doors, to welcome strangers who will leave as friends, and to embark on an adventure that is as rewarding as it is challenging.

So, brew yourself a cup of tea or coffee, find a cozy nook, and let us begin this journey together. Your future as a bed and breakfast owner awaits, and I promise, it is a journey worth taking.

2

The Bed and Breakfast – A World of Differences

To the untrained eye, a bed and breakfast might seem like just another lodging option, a cousin to hotels and motels scattered across the highways and byways. But, oh, how mistaken that view is! A bed and breakfast is not just a place to rest your weary head; it is an experience, a personal journey, a story waiting to unfold with each new guest. And this is from someone, your author, who spent exactly four nights at three bed and breakfasts in my entire life! Hard to believe, huh?

So, what exactly sets a bed and breakfast apart from its more commercial cousins, the inns, hotels, and motels of the world? It is akin to comparing a home-cooked meal with a fast-food dinner. Both serve the basic purpose of nourishing, but the similarities end there.

At its heart, a bed and breakfast is a private home with a character all its own, where guests are welcomed not just as customers but as valued visitors. It is often run by individuals or families, passionate about hospitality and eager to share their home and experiences. These establishments typically have a handful of rooms, each with a private bathroom (American tourists expect this.), and are uniquely decorated, offering a level of comfort and personality that larger hotels can only dream of.

The "bed" in bed and breakfast is more than just a place to sleep; it is a haven. Imagine rooms adorned with quilted bedspreads, antique furniture, and perhaps a gentle creak in the floorboards - an audible reminder of the history and charm of the place. And then there is the "breakfast" part - a feast for the senses, often homemade and shared around a communal table, providing not just sustenance but a chance to connect, share stories, talk about their experience as a tourist in the area, and maybe even laugh at a local joke or two.

In contrast, other inns or lodges, while charming in their way, often miss this personal touch. They are businesses first and foremost, designed for efficiency, standardization, and volume. Their rooms, though comfortable, lack the individual personality of a bed and breakfast. They cater to the traveler who seeks predictability and anonymity - which, don't get me wrong, has its place. But it is a different melody altogether.

The magic of a bed and breakfast lies not just in its physical comforts but in its ability to create a sense of belonging and connection. It is like staying with a friend - a friend who happens to make an excellent blueberry pancake and can tell you the best spot to catch the sunset. This personal touch extends beyond decor and meals; it is in the very essence of the experience. Innkeepers often serve as local guides, historians, and sometimes, if the need arises, sympathetic listeners.

Each bed and breakfast also reflects the personality and interests of its owners. You might find yourself in a Victorian-era mansion steeped in history, a rustic cabin surrounded by wilderness, an old farmhouse built in 1872 that sits in the mountains and overflows with fascinating history, or a modern abode adorned with contemporary art. This variety is the spice of the bed and breakfast world, ensuring that no two visits, even to the same region, are ever quite the same.

The bed and breakfast can be and usually serves as a cultural touchstone in the area. These establishments often preserve historical buildings and local traditions, providing a window into the past and a connection to the local community. They are not just places to stay; they are custodians of stories and traditions, passing them on to each new guest.

In conclusion, a bed and breakfast is more than a lodging option; it is a choice to experience travel through a more intimate, personal lens. It is about embracing the unique, the quirky, the homespun. It is about choosing connection over convenience, and stories over standardization.

As we venture further into this book, remember that the essence of a bed and breakfast is not just in its beds or its breakfasts, but in the memories it creates, the comfort it provides, and the stories it tells. And who knows? By the end of this journey, you might find yourself not just staying in one but dreaming of running your own.

Next up, we will explore the first crucial steps in setting up your bed and breakfast. Buckle up; it is going to be an exciting ride!

3

Laying the Foundations –Preparing to Open Your Bed and Breakfast

I magine standing before an empty canvas, brush in hand, ready to create a masterpiece. This is precisely where we find ourselves as we prepare to open a bed and breakfast. It is an exciting, slightly daunting task, akin to preparing for a grand party where the guests are yet to arrive, and the decorations are still in boxes.

1. Finding the Perfect Location: The Charm of Place

The first stroke on our canvas is location. A good location for a bed and breakfast is like finding the perfect backdrop for our masterpiece. It's not just about being in a popular area; it is about finding a place with a special appeal, a character that will resonate with your future guests. Is it nestled in a quaint village, perched by the seaside, or tucked away in a forest glen? Each setting tells a different story and will attract a different kind of guest.

2. Decorating with Purpose: Creating an Ambiance

Once you've found the right location, the next step is to infuse it with personality - your personality. Decorating is not just about aesthetics; it is about creating an ambiance that complements the location's appeal. Each room should tell its own story, be it through antique furniture, modern art, or cozy fabrics. This is where your personal touch transforms a house into a home for your guests. Each room will showcase its unique name, a name that you have bestowed upon it. It now has its own character with your touches and your ambiance.

3. The Legalities: Licenses and Insurance

Before the dream can take flight, there are practicalities to consider. Securing a business license is crucial; it is the formal attire for your bed and breakfast, ensuring that everything is legitimate and above board. Then there is insurance - not the most thrilling chapter in our story, but perhaps one of the most important. Insurance, including both structure and liability, is the safety net that lets you sleep peacefully at night, knowing that both you and your guests are protected.

In most jurisdictions, you will have a local Health Department that will be reviewing your facility and giving you specific information about food prep, cleanliness, and ensuring that you have met the legal requirements. This is very important to your success and your ability to open the facility to guests! Make sure that you follow the rules and prove to the health inspectors that you are a serious innkeeper who will follow their suggestions and rules. You call them and ask to meet them and welcome a visit to your B & B if they have not already been in contact. Do this well before you open.

4. The Business Plan: Charting Your Course

"A business without a plan is like a boat without a rudder," as the old saying goes. Crafting a business plan might not stir the soul, but it is essential. It is your map, guiding you through the financial waters, helping you understand your market, setting realistic goals, and managing your finances. Professional help can be invaluable here, turning a daunting task into a manageable one.

5. The Practicalities: Bed, Breakfast, and Beyond

Finally, it is time to think about the bread and butter of your enterprise – literally. Beds need to be comfortable; breakfasts need to be memorable, and the experience needs to be seamless. This means thinking about everything from the fluffiness of your pillows to the variety of your menu, from the warmth of your welcome to the efficiency of your booking system.

Opening a bed and breakfast is a journey that combines the heart's passion with the mind's practicalities. It is about creating a space that feels like a home and runs like a business. It is about being ready to welcome your first guests with open arms and a well-prepared plan.

In the next chapter, we will delve into the art of creating that perfect guest experience, from the moment they step through your door to the heartfelt goodbye. It is where the magic happens, where your bed and breakfast comes to life. So, let us turn the page and continue our journey into the heart of bed and breakfast hospitality - the guest experience. This chapter is not just about hospitality though; it is about creating connections, moments, and memories that guests will cherish long after they have returned home. It is about turning first-time visitors into lifelong friends and advocates for your charming retreat.

4

The Art of Guest Satisfaction —Cultivating Memorable Experiences

Always, always, always be the first person to greet your guests. I would watch their car drive in, see them exit the car, and head to the house. They were sometimes excited to be here and sometimes nervous, not knowing what to expect. It was my job to allay the anxiety and set the tone for them! That tone will carry on throughout their entire stay.

1. First Impressions: The Power of a Good Introduction

As the adage goes, you never get a second chance to make a first impression. Your introduction to guests sets the tone for their entire stay. It is not just about a friendly smile (though that certainly helps); it is about conveying warmth, professionalism, and a genuine interest in their well-being. This is where you step into the role of host, guide, and sometimes even storyteller, welcoming your guests not just to your establishment but to an experience.

2. The Art of Listening: Understanding Your Guests

One of the most underrated skills in hospitality is the ability to listen. It is more than just hearing the words; it is understanding the unspoken needs and expectations of your guests. Are they here to relax, to experience a new adventure, to "get away from the kids" for a weekend, or all of the above? Listening attentively not only helps you tailor their experience but also makes your guests feel valued and understood. Listen well.

3. Engagement: Asking the Right Questions

Building rapport with guests is like nurturing a garden - it requires care, attention, and the right environment to flourish. Engaging with guests through thoughtful questions helps unearth common interests, preferences, and expectations. This engagement not only enhances their stay but also deepens their connection with you and your bed and breakfast.

4. Respect and Welcome: The Cornerstones of Hospitality

Respect and welcome are the cornerstones of any successful hospitality venture. They go beyond mere politeness; they are about creating an environment where guests feel safe, valued, and cared for. This means respecting their privacy, catering to their needs, and always being available to assist, advise, or simply share a warm conversation.

5. Personal Touch: The Guest as a Friend

In the world of bed and breakfasts, guests are not just clients; they are friends you have not met yet. Treating each guest as your newest friend creates a personal and intimate experience that large hotels can rarely match. This approach fosters loyalty, repeat visits, and word-of-mouth recommendations.

6. The Magic of Names: A Simple but Powerful Tool

Remembering and using a guest's name is a simple yet powerful tool for building a connection. It is a small gesture that has an enormous impact, making guests feel recognized and important. It is the thread that weaves the tapestry of personal touch throughout their stay.

In this chapter, we have explored the nuances of developing clientele satisfaction in a bed and breakfast setting. It is the little things - a warm greeting, a listening ear, and a personal touch - that transform a good stay into a memorable one.

As we move forward, we will delve into the practical aspects of running your bed and breakfast. We will cover some of the essentials that keep the wheels turning smoothly at your charming inn. Let us continue our journey into creating not just a business, but a haven for those who seek it.

.

5

Cultivating Loyalty –The Art of Building Repeat Business

I n the enchanting world of bed and breakfasts, repeat business is not just a segment of your revenue; it is the heart and soul of your enterprise. It is the warm smile of a returning guest, the shared stories that have grown a little since last time, and the sense of familiarity and belonging that grows with every visit. In this chapter, we explore turning first-time visitors into lifelong guests.

1. Crafting a Memorable Experience: Beyond the Ordinary

Creating a memorable experience for your guests is like painting a masterpiece that stays with them long after they have left. It is more than just comfortable beds and delicious breakfasts; it is creating moments of delight and surprise. It is the freshly baked cookies in the afternoon, the hand-drawn map of hidden local gems, or the cozy reading nook that beckons with a selection of books. These experiences do not just satisfy guests; they enchant them. Your observations of their wishes make a big difference in their experience! You can count on it.

2. The Power of Presence: Mingling in Common Areas

Your presence as an innkeeper is a vital ingredient in the guest experience. Mingling with guests in shared areas isn't just being available for questions; it shows genuine interest and warmth. Share stories, ask about their day, or simply offer a listening ear. This personal interaction adds depth to their stay that impersonal lodgings cannot match.

3. Fostering Local Connections: Become a Community Hub

Building relationships with local businesses is a strategy with a dual benefit. Not only do you provide your guests with quality recommendations, enhancing their experience, but you also become a part of a network where local businesses support and refer each other. From the local florist to the corner café, these connections embed your bed and breakfast in the fabric of the community.

Additionally, join the local Chamber of Commerce and other business organizations and clubs in your community. Get on the Board of Directions of some of these organizations. Make friends. Give back. They will refer your B & B over and over again when the opportunity avails itself. The opportunity is well worth the relatively small investment of time and money on your part,

4. Community Engagement: The Art of Giving Back

Engaging with your community is more than business; it is about belonging. Donate nights for local charity events, sponsor community gatherings, or participate in local festivals. These acts of community integration do more than just get your name out there; they weave your bed and breakfast into the community's narrative, making you a cherished local landmark rather than just a place to stay.

5. A Parting Gift: Encouraging Return Visits

As your guests prepare to leave, a small gesture can go a long way. A parting gift, a personalized thank-you note, or an offer for a special rate on their next stay can leave an impression. It is a final flourish that says,

"You're more than a guest; you are part of our story."

In this chapter, we have explored the rich tapestry of strategies that transform first-time guests into returning friends. It is a blend of memorable experiences, personal connections, community integration, and thoughtful gestures. Your bed and breakfast is a living story; share it with your wonderful and cherished guests!

6

The Joy of Connection –Enjoying the Company of Your Guests

I n the heartwarming narrative of running a bed and breakfast, the chapter on enjoying the company of your guests is the most fulfilling. This is not merely providing a service; it is opening your world to others and, in turn, becoming a part of theirs. In this chapter, we explore how to make the most of these interactions, creating a tapestry of shared stories, laughter, and genuine connections.

1. Making Interactions Special: The Personal Touch

Each interaction with your guests is an opportunity to make their stay memorable. It is the small gestures that often leave the deepest impression – a personalized welcome note, a thoughtful recommendation for a day trip, or just taking the time to chat over a cup of coffee. These moments are the essence of the bed and breakfast experience, setting you apart from the impersonal nature of larger hotels.

2. Sharing Your Stories: The Lifeblood of Your B&B

Every bed and breakfast has its stories, and sharing these with your guests can be both entertaining and endearing. Whether it is the history of your property, the tale of how you became an innkeeper, or amusing anecdotes from your experiences, these stories breathe life into your

B&B. They transform it from a mere place to stay into a living, breathing character in your guests' travel stories.

3. Embracing the Humorous: Laughter as a Bonding Tool

Humor is a universal language and sharing the funny side of B&B life can be a delightful way to bond with your guests. Whether it is a quirky habit of a local resident, a comical mishap in the kitchen, or a playful interaction with a pet, laughter creates a sense of ease and camaraderie. It is these light-hearted moments that often lead to lasting friendships and repeat visits.

4. Authenticity: Inviting Guests into Your World

The most important aspect of enjoying your guests' company is simply being yourself. Authenticity is magnetic; when you are genuine in your interactions, guests feel more relaxed and welcome. Invite them into your world, and share your passions, your dreams, and your journey. This authenticity creates a deep and meaningful connection that transcends the typical guest-host relationship.

5. Creating a Community of Guests

Your bed and breakfast can become more than just a collection of rooms; it can be a community. Encourage interaction among guests – over communal breakfasts or complimentary evening gatherings with hors d'oeuvres and wine. This not only enhances their experience but also creates a network of connections, making their stay at your B&B memorable and unique. How about a Mystery Night, a who-done-it experience your guests will enjoy and keep as an exciting memory to share with friends and relatives when they return home?

In this chapter, we have embraced the joy and art of connecting with guests, turning each stay into a shared experience. As we turn to the next chapter, we will explore the practical side of managing these relationships, from handling feedback to ensuring that each guest leaves with a desire to return. Your bed and breakfast is more than a business; it's a stage for shared stories and a haven for creating new ones. Let us continue to nurture these connections as we move forward.

As we turn the page to the next chapter, we will delve into the digital world of managing your online presence and using technology to enhance guest experiences and streamline operations. This can and should be an exciting and meaningful part of your business. Enjoy it!

7

The Marquee of Success –Marketing your Bed and Breakfast

Welcome to the digital marquee of the 21st century, where marketing your bed and breakfast becomes an art form, blending the charm of your establishment with the savvy of modern advertising techniques. In this chapter, we delve into the world of marketing, exploring how to display your unique heaven to the world while maintaining its authentic charm. It is well worth the effort you put in.

1. Crafting Your Digital Front Porch: Your Website

Imagine your website as the digital front porch of your bed and breakfast. It is the first impression potential guests will have, and it needs to be inviting. A catchy, easy-to-navigate website that encapsulates the essence of your B&B is crucial. Ensure it has stunning photos, compelling descriptions, and easy links to booking and inquiries. Think of it as a virtual tour, one that entices visitors to step through your actual front door. Add some soothing music to the site as your potential guests explore; let their emotional and soothing feelings come to life.

2. Social Media: Building Your Online Community

Social media is like the town square of the digital age, a place to

Gather, share stories, and connect. But remember, it is not just being present; it is being relevant. Tailor your social media presence to match the interests and ages of your typical guests. Share glimpses of daily life at your B&B, from the morning mist over the garden to the evening lights in the dining room. Engage with your followers, answer questions, and create a sense of community around your brand.

3. Networking with Peers: Joining Associations

Joining statewide bed and breakfast associations is like becoming part of a larger family. These associations offer a wealth of resources, from marketing opportunities to valuable networking. Attend meetings, participate in forums, and get to know your fellow B&B owners. Often, these connections lead to referrals, shared wisdom, and friendships that enrich both your personal life and your business.

4. The Magic of Storytelling: Videos and Virtual Experiences

In an age where content is king, creating engaging videos can be your royal flush. Whether it is a virtual tour of your B&B, a glimpse into your kitchen preparations, or something more whimsical like local legends and ghost stories, videos can capture the imagination of potential guests. Share these videos on your website, social media, and even through email newsletters. They are not just marketing tools; they are invitations to experience a story - your story.

5. Consistency and Creativity: The Marketing Balance

Remember, the key to successful marketing is a balance between consistency and creativity. Keep your branding consistent across all platforms, but do not be afraid to try new things. Whether it is a seasonal promotion, a special event, or a unique package deal, these efforts keep your marketing fresh and engaging. Even your name is a brand. My brand name was "Doc" and to many people I still am. It served me well as everyone called me by that name from guests to community members! I suspect that many people in the community still do not know my given name!

In this chapter, we have navigated the exciting world of marketing your bed and breakfast. It is more than just selling a room; it is selling an experience, a dream, a temporary home. As you turn your attention to the "end game" of living the dream in the next chapter, remember that every marketing effort is a brushstroke in the larger picture of your business' success. Let us continue to paint that picture together.

8

Living the Dream –Embracing the Bed and Breakfast Lifestyle

And now, we arrive at the heart of our story, the chapter where the essence of running a bed and breakfast shines brightest.

This is not just a business venture; it is a lifestyle choice, a dream woven from threads of hospitality, warmth, and joy. In this chapter, we celebrate the fulfillment that comes from not only achieving your dream but living it every day.

1. The Reward of Happiness: Seeing Your Guests Smile

There is a unique satisfaction in seeing the happiness of your guests, knowing it is you and your bed and breakfast that has brought joy to them. Whether it is seeing them relax in the garden or front porch, hearing their laughter at breakfast, conducting a marriage renewal underneath a large oak in your yard, or reading a heartfelt note they have left behind, these moments are affirmations of your dream. They are reminders of why you embarked on this journey - to make people happy, to create a space of comfort and joy.

2. Embodying Positivity: Being the Happy Host

As the face and soul of your bed and breakfast, your mood sets the tone. Embrace the role of the happy host, not just as a business strategy,

3. The Art of Self-Care: Keeping the Dream Alive

While caring for your guests, it is vital to remember to care for yourself. Living the dream means finding a balance between your role as an innkeeper and your well-being. Take time to enjoy your passions, relax in your favorite nook of the B&B, or explore your surroundings. A happy, well-rested host is the cornerstone of a thriving bed and breakfast.

4. Continuous Improvement: Growing with Your Dream

Living the dream is an evolving journey. It is continuously finding ways to enhance your B&B and your own experience as an innkeeper. Attend workshops, connect with other B&B owners, and gather feedback from guests. Use these insights to refine and grow your dream, keeping it vibrant and fulfilling.

5. Sharing the Joy: Spreading the Word

As you live and breathe your dream, share your journey with others. Whether through social media, a blog, or casual conversations with guests, let people see the joy and passion behind your B&B. Your story is not just inspiring; it is a testament to the attainability of dreams.

In this chapter, we have embraced the essence of living the dream of owning and running a bed and breakfast. It is a journey marked by smiles, shared stories, and the joy of creating a haven for others. As you turn the pages of your own story each day, remember that your bed and breakfast is more than a business; it is a dream made real, a canvas of experiences, and a home of memories for both you and your guests.

And there you have it, a sneak peek into the world of Bed and Breakfasts through the eyes of someone who's been there, done that, and got the apron to prove it. "INN LOVE" is your go-to guide, a friend in the form of a book, waiting to accompany you on this exhilarating journey.

Be creative. Do what guests would never expect at those "other" hospitality businesses. I give you permission to have fun! You and your guests will enjoy the once-in-a-lifetime experience.

As we close this chapter, we look forward to the continuous journey ahead, filled with new guests, new stories, and the enduring warmth of your bed and breakfast dream. Keep living the dream, for it is not just yours, but a shared dream with every guest who walks through your door.

Get out your best apron and turn that dream into a reality.   Doc

9

Conclusion and Reference

I t has been a joy to write this introduction to the B & B business! As I think back to 2006-2018 when I opened and operated my Bed and Breakfast, I cannot help but wonder how I learned the business with so few nights (four to be exact) as a guest myself at three other Bed and Breakfasts. I think I just might have had some *special* help along the way to figure things out. I sincerely hope that the ideas and suggestions I have written for you will be that catalyst and beginning support system to help you build the business and develop many friendships at your B & B. May these ideas and suggestions be some of *your special help along the way*. Doc

Reference

OpenAI. (2023). ChatGPT. https://openai.com/chatgpt

10

Keeping the Dream Alive

Congratulations on completing this journey! You now have the knowledge and inspiration to start your own bed and breakfast adventure. It's time to share this gift with others.

By leaving your honest review of this book on Amazon, you can guide fellow aspiring innkeepers to the **same** valuable insights you've discovered. Your opinion matters and can light the way for others who share your passion for hospitality. See the QR code below.

Thank you for being a part of keeping the dream of innkeeping alive. Our community grows stronger with each story shared and each dream realized.

Together, we're not just running inns; we're building a world of warmth, welcome, and wonder.

Let's keep the dream alive, one review at a time.

About the Author

After working 30 years in public school education in Florida (11 in teaching and 19 in district-level administration) I decided to retire in June of 2006. By then I had already purchased my home/bed and breakfast in the mountains of North Carolina, and I returned it to its original 1870s charm! I virtually started the business without having much knowledge about the B and B day-to-day operations, but just decided that I would forge ahead anyway. Overall, I had a great time sitting on the front porch looking at the mountains, greeting guests, making and serving breakfasts, showing guests to their rooms, and getting involved in the community. I never looked back and enjoyed the decade-plus one year as a very happy innkeeper. Brian "Doc" Adams

www.ingramcontent.com/pod-product-compliance
Lightning Source LLC
Chambersburg PA
CBHW071020290526
45795CB00005B/1874